Naked Feathers

Martha

Many pleasant moments of reading and I thank god for sending your friendship to me - which can not be bought at any price, but lunch at Danielle's was great!

Diane B.

Naked Feathers

Diane Bostick

iUniverse, Inc.
New York Lincoln Shanghai

Naked Feathers

Copyright © 2006 by Diane Bostick

All rights reserved. No part of this book may be used or reproduced by any means, graphic, electronic, or mechanical, including photocopying, recording, taping or by any information storage retrieval system without the written permission of the publisher except in the case of brief quotations embodied in critical articles and reviews.

iUniverse books may be ordered through booksellers or by contacting:

iUniverse
2021 Pine Lake Road, Suite 100
Lincoln, NE 68512
www.iuniverse.com
1-800-Authors (1-800-288-4677)

ISBN-13: 978-0-595-40083-6 (pbk)
ISBN-13: 978-0-595-84467-8 (ebk)
ISBN-10: 0-595-40083-3 (pbk)
ISBN-10: 0-595-84467-7 (ebk)

Printed in the United States of America

Contents

PIGEONS 1
ACTING 2
SUMMER 3
BRASS BAND 4
MOTORS OF MY HEART 5
GONE FROGGING 6
A COWBOY NAMED DAVE 8
NIGHTMARES 10
ON A BIKE 11
AUNT MARGIE'S ODE 12
SELF DEFENSE 13
DETAILS 14
NEW SPRINGS 15
SNAKE PEOPLE 16
SUNRISE IN KOREA 18
STOP HEART 19
PUT IT IN THE MUSIC 20
THE ASSEMBLY LINE 21
ONLY GIRL 22
ANSWERING EMILY 22
SCARS 24
DAY OF THE PROPHETS 25
IDES 26
IT WASN'T 27
SMOKING 28
MOTHER STORIES 30

THE TREE FELLER	31
RENOVATIONS	32
MORNINGS' MAGIC	33
SIX DAYS IN PARIS, TONIGHT	34
LEAVES	36
I'M A TENNIS RACKET	37
FIRESIDE CHATS	38
THE BLACK SQUIRREL	39
THE CAT	40
PURPLE ROOT BEER	42
SUBURBAN POLAR BEAR	43
SHIP OF LOVE	44
SEPARATION	46
UMBRELLAS IN THE SUN	47
HOMESPUN VIEW	48
THE DISGUISE	50
RIVERSIDE	52
WELL PRESERVED	53
BEHIND BINOCULARS	54
SCENTS	55
CARNIVAL RAIN	56
WHEN I THINK OF YOU	58
RIVALS	59
THE DUTIES OF A QUEEN	60
ENTER MY SOUL	62
FOUR WALLS AND A CEILING	64
NAKED FEATHERS	65
GIVE ME BACK MY HEART	66
EVERY LANGUAGE	67
THE UN-OPENING	68
GETTING OFF THE GROUND	69

PIGEONS

Every night, I seek that pigeon
From my window on the stair—
Sitting, like she's knitting
In her window, creviced, lair
The winds blow cold and quiet—
Making naked feathers whirl—
Guarding as she does, three eggs—
With body aptly curled.

I'd like to help her in her task—
Of scouting sticks and twine—
How little does she know, how much
Her life resembles mine?

ACTING

I wonder, as I live my life
on borrowed phrases—
what wonderful scenes
I may be missing
under the sun—
where people are suntanned
and smell of ignorance
while I remember fallen roses
from opening nights
I wonder
as I glance into the pale
of footlight hands
what fantasy of mine
will brilliantly live
only to die away
crash, like a reckless, unloved
starling
and briefly, I clamor
for simple domestic fevers
quiet hours of untold days of
ordinary loving
made bold by merely living
in the scrupulous shadow
of muffled and lazy things.
I wonder
without speeches
of simpler, less demanding kisses
made quiet through consistent
familiarity
without props
or extra dashes of rouge
and nothing to call me away for.
I no longer need worry of wrinkles
I have earned them
fair and square—
from the best of the dead.

SUMMER

Hazy heat of yesterday's rain—
Heaped on streets of sun glassed people.

Filling my nostrils, Dizzying my head
Widening my heart.

Unforgivable, Old reliable—
Summer

BRASS BAND

little black boys
run the circle round
the splattering city fountain,
on concrete edge

repeating, beneath the sun
the songs of heat and sweat
creeping out of worn sneakers

cursing back to one another
in a special language
lunging like heavy summer birds
restless in the sound wave
the Park Mobile's brass band

MOTORS OF MY HEART

Racing the motors of my heart
you step in gear
and I hear doubt descending
in its place along our sides

but something in the speeding
lends an air of slight
sharp vagrancy
cornering me with countless, lucid
demonic kisses
the summer sun had given us

then shifting back to roads that
gage the golden mileage
in tears

GONE FROGGING

Frogs were dancing in the light of crooked stars
    Moonlit, croaking for a piece of lily pad—
I swore that they were good with love
        And princes rare—
How tainted was my disbelief in fairy tales
    As I arrive on dragonfly to check the wares—

  Blown cheeks like sticky bubble gum
      And tongues that swept like lightening in
          the dewy air—
     They sniffed me like an insect and then
        winked at me, and sighing, took me dancing
  in the fading night.
    I dreamed of wind and willows much more civilized
      And left all emptied like a dried out lily pad.

One night the stars were straighter and the dancers-few
    I felt the world was fresh that night
        I tossed my shoes to race beyond the buggy swamp
          For fireflies
(As I look back, I realize how very wise)

  A brand new band was pumping out new fairy tales
        And on the light of moonbeams dreams came flying down
    The ugliest of frogs moved princely to the sound
      With elegance reborn—All poets made like clowns

Without a space to hide, I hid among the weeds
    And dug the mud for treasures
  In my rolled up sleeves.
Band masters all applauded my triumphant stance
  unlikely princes begged me for steady dance

Then thru a whisper, you, the price (Unlikeliest of all)
    had lost your crown, like Cinderella lost her dress
and asked me if the dragonfly was up for sale and

   if the dance was taken and
  why was I so pale?

You couldn't be a frog,
   Your eyes too sweet and clean
And I wondered how a creature like you
      wound up here

I wrapped my hand in yours
    —the music fit our steps
we talked below the surface to the deepest depths
  and onward—until two years caught up with us.

Though the mist has faded—
   So too the frogs have passed, and so
We too have ended, though the memory lasts

I'll never judge a swamp again the same
    since I loved you—the greatest frog of love
       who had my soul, renewed.

A COWBOY NAMED DAVE

There's a town in Wyoming
   that's dusty and dark
with a history of sin-filled desire

—An outpost for outlaws
not too long ago
   filled with wranglers who ought to retire

In a bar on the wall
       hang wild antelope heads
  and Old Walt plays his favorite tune

It's a nice place to play
       if you like the romance
  of a 20th century saloon

And all of the town folk will tell you
   a body don't need to behave
cause there's many a woman has walked in the Drifter's
   and left with a cowboy named "Dave"

The same time each day (or a little bit later)
   a rambler will move through the door
  you'll swear that that's something so different about him
    but swear that you've seen him before

A Black Stetson hat floats above his blue eyes
    that go staring right through you and back,
a Silver Tongued Devil soon forces his hand
      and he drawls that he knows where it's at

And while he is spending he a drink
    or three on her
he's spending the dreams that she saved
  but there's many a woman has walked through the Drifter's
    and left with a cowboy named Dave

The Drifiter's is closing up, 3 every morning—
    so most folks crack up or go home
but the last one still sitting, is sliding and slipping
    some young thing that came there alone

And while he repeats all the lines he had jotted
    right down on the wall of his head—
they both know it's time to make good of the moonlight
    where dreams and their devils make friends

And there's no one to blame and there's nothing to lose
    but a feeling for love they both crave
and there's no one who drifts through the Drifters knows better
    than a sweet talking cowboy named Dave

NIGHTMARES

We need not live with nightmares—
They're just part-time guests;
Sad mysteries and histories
We choose to play

I'd rather tie some dreams down
To a jagged earth—
Than hang on to a nightmare
That has lost its shine.

What need to be a wandering ghost
In houses we have left;
When to catch a falling leaf—
We hold the universe.

Nightmares are just wishes
Where a horse should be—
We need to ride into daylight
Where our hearts ride free.

ON A BIKE

On my wheels made of wings—
    there are no finer things
        than
the sun-melted greens of the trees;
        I will glide though the air
      where magicians don't dare,

leaving traces of glow from my eyes—
    While peddling on
        through the dusk of a dream

I shall witness the last of the sky.

AUNT MARGIE'S ODE

the day we, dress to suit
gave Margie rights—
some flowers smiled to welcome her
and I wondered why we couldn't stay
to watch them cover her

back there, the cold, stone altar
looked uncomfortable,
in tripping on the steps,
I scraped my consciousness—
I smelled the gladioli, in embarrassment
and wondered why
I couldn't kiss her cheek

the sun nodded through
most helplessly
in that stiff, groomed air
while words, doused with bereavement
soon were lost
beneath her plot
and mother cried for her sister Marge
and I wondered if god heard it, all the way up there
or if he made a different noise from us

and as we drove away to go to lunch
my eyes dried clear, my heart was straight
my hunger stretched in the shine of
a black limousine
when I looked back and saw
the flowers smile to welcome her
I wondered if their roots—planted deep
could hold her closer there—
than ever in our eager grasp
would we.

SELF DEFENSE

When fusion is a weakness
and you can't see the mistakes
you're making
for the embraces—
then you turn off the light
you exercise restraint
as you would walk a dog.
So then love
lost or found
follows in its place;
an old letter, that, at last
you can tear
a new lover that, at last
you can be wary of—
think of walking, dogs and rain,
and carry an umbrella
for your soul.

DETAILS

How strange
   to wake
   to something missing in
the morning

Between the empty sounds
   of breakfast made for one
      the droning TV news
         that breaks your brain out like a
           shell shorn egg

singular feelings
   of missed connection:
   though in a glance
      all seems in place

not asking anymore
   how to live
but simply to do morning
   til afternoon finds you and
      evening disguises loneliness till ten

how warm to wake to kisses
    I'd forgotten
nothing missing but morning
    from the mourning

gladly to let another set of eyes
   be the news
another pair of hands
    to paint the starting light
       gathering with ease into night

how foolish to have missed
   so simple a detail; as, love.

NEW SPRINGS

Melting winter, you softly come
into Spring in the night

and from my porch—
afraid to move too much

to lose that crisp and still remaining
snow air

I watch, removed from time
to nowhere I remember

a part of you,
apart from other souls

and quiet glossy streets of water,
where smooth ice once lay,
reflect a strange fulfillment of

your change and mine.

SNAKE PEOPLE

Back in the days of the panoramic
    projector camera thing
  and when Dr. Spock knew it all;

we were let to follow our hearts
    as children.
My brother was a member of the
    snake of the month club,

before reptile cruelty laws—
    they came in the mailbox
  wrapped in a gauze bag,
      or a box of some sort,
        and they would go into our basement,
          in various makeshift cages;
also, the laundry room was down there
    needless to say, snakes can't stay put

  but perhaps it was a blessing
      in my shorts one day I found only a rat snake
  not an Anaconda.

We did not get the Anaconda or the Python,
    because you needed a special license and
        we had far too many young children and
          cats and dogs in the neighborhood.

    but occasionally got a free horned toad;

  these were not convenient because they
    spit blood, and one time at 11,
      I thought I was starting my period two years too early.

Mother's thoughts were perhaps
    for no other reason snakes were good—
      to control the rodent population,

and keep our nosy neighbor,
       Mr. Snelling, away from the door

  he had a noisy and very nervous poodle,
     for that reason we often pined
         that we could not own the Python.

To make it short—my brother, snake man
   was my only friend—
when very small I followed him until
    it was very inconvenient
       having baby sister around

and he left me to find my own friends, during the snake era
   I could only follow the shedding skins, and
      find the runaways in my underwear,

and feed squirrels in the back yard.
There is something to be said of
    a household that grooms snakes;
      a feel for reptiles,
I never had children myself, to comfort me in older age;
     but
   I am now the proud owner of
      snake purses, belts and shoes boutique.
Some of brother's snakes that went missing were never found.

SUNRISE IN KOREA

She held out the letter
    the seal was colored army green
A-1 status, for her lover
    just teenage dreams had she

Her eyes grew cloudy, tears fell
    for wedding bells were overdue—
coming of age isn't easy
    in the land of the free—paying dues

When is sunshine in Korea?
    can we send coffee, candy, tears?
will he find a roadside flower,
    like the one that's dying here?

She shined his boots the brightest
    and they shaved his head completely
he took his shots and training
    so her love grew much more sweetly

One day while it was raining,
    her heart stopped once and then again
he waved from one small window
    in the shadow of a plane

He hung his hat at An-Jun-Ni
    one day the letter came
new lovers found her, took his place
    he couldn't find the tears

The stash he kept, he opened up
    once put aside for her
til days turned into weeks
    —the world, a dizzy blur

When is Sunrise in Korea?
    this nations hope grew dim
the boy, a man, his spirit dull
    his love misplacing him.

STOP HEART

Stop heart
on a dime
it's about time
back to a place before the games—sooth
where the fever is hottest
reclaim the land of trust
just stop heart—you indecent fool
don't burn away to dust
don't tell me you could lie after all this time
Stop heart
on a dime
it's past time
Let me, let me, let me
Love again.

PUT IT IN THE MUSIC

The spotlight takes it's own sweet time—
    it doesn't care if you are fine,
there's other faces, left to shine
      before they fade away

It wouldn't be so bad to feel
   if everything they say is real—
but every truth you've got to steal.
     there's people in the way

Put it in the music
   I don't want to lose it,
Put it in the music,
   It's the happy way

Walking down the empty street
   there's no one left you'd like to meet
     you play alone, it feels so sweet
the night is yours to take

Put it in the music
   I don't want to lose it
Put it in the music
   It's the happy way
     The happy way

THE ASSEMBLY LINE

faces smile but share no bond with me
as slow, clock hands
imitate mine
without expression, or sound

consumed in the solder smoke
of hot brass joints,
be goggled, we bend the coils
three turn
in the smell of cigarettes from break

sweating underneath the foreman—
stern and brush cut
hearing our gossip
he stops-he moves
we sit alone, side by side
feisty tinkers
trading whispered jokes
but smiling
when bells ring

ONLY GIRL
By Emily Bostick 2006

My only girl—
   though your hair would not curl!—
bright of mind—
   and quick of step—
full of vim and vigor—
   and chock full of pop!!

ANSWERING EMILY

I swing upon
your swift moving legs—
as you fly room to room

your ready smile and blonde mane
help me not grow up too soon

for like a child
adventure came to you
to pass along

your eyes as bright as any child
your spirit, wrapped in song

far away but still so real—
I recall moments here
For you stayed North
while I moved south—
now, childhood shines more clear

Your soft firm hands
then larger, than mine
pulled me round big objects
time after time

Long into day
with my brother and I
you whipped supper fast
then allowed TV time

while still wrapped in excitement
you gathered the books
for your guided word tour
with expressions that shook

Though I hung on your voice
as I skipped off to sleep
with the world in my head
and sweet tones of your speech.

And you let me watch ants
and play in the sand
often in the park
beside me you ran—

you were wind, and wise sayings
and once a tap dancer

When I bunch up from thought—
you relieve with soft answers

Now that I'm grown
and I run through my sand
you are pacing me still
those memories in hand

Breaking miles into laps—
I do more for the hip
which has kept you tame
since that time when you slipped

Still you cheer from the benches
and walk fast as able
and when holidays come
yours still the best table

So now, growing on—
I'm bound to remember

Where you brought me to life in
that special November.

SCARS

I have mine inside my body
yours displayed across your heart;
patchwork stitches
where they went to save you—

I've been beaten on the outside,
bruises left
like the brown on bananas
across my arms and around eyes

though they have faded
your scars are not forgotten

my scars rock through me
as ghosts of the past
unpredictable, ready to strike

yours are a warning
take it easy

mine the eternal guests
urged to keep the lid on

when I touch your scars
I feel them fade

I wish I knew the way
to keep the lid on me

You hold me close
I forget inside

maybe we are one
two layers of skin
that need to heal
together

DAY OF THE PROPHETS

Wake up to a golden, clear morning—
   wrap up cause they say it will rain—
watch out cause a new day is dawning,
    prophets are preaching, but what do they say?

High rises get closer to heaven,
    Pent houses, but no one can hide
good place to shoot dice of sevens
    plan out those speeches to heal the blind

Gather sick, gather sinners
   argue rights, argue wrongs
cause the day of the prophets has never looked
   better
   the day of the prophets has come

You want a new face, you can buy one
   a body, with botox, new brain
watch tv when your day is through
     take pills for the pain

Gather sick, gather sinners
   argue rights, argue wrongs
cause the day of the prophets has never looked
   better
   the day of the prophets has come

Slow down, when you sit at the wheel
    turn down the noise of the hour
think fast, once you get on your feet
    the hero's religion is feeding on power

Gathering sick, gathering sinner
   arguing rights, argue wrongs
the day of the prophets has never looked
   better, the day of the prophets has come.

IDES

I haven't the fire
   of my mother's Irish
I am content to stare at
     the blizzard
and near the ice veined panes
    stand in the sweet smell
       of last night's brandy—
to watch the bar sign across the street
   swing in the white Ides of March ;
     to let the morning paper keep itself

at the corner store.

The jig I know best
   is the quiet sleeping off of winter
     and my blarnish hero is McMurphy—
  for he too had his
    private cuckoo's nest.

with your glass in my hand—
  I pray for the thaw
  and count on a shamrocked Spring.

IT WASN'T

It wasn't what I thought;
   a laughter, taking me by surprise,
  layered
        with a simple recipe for satisfying needs;
 cradled at the bottom of an old
        box of dreams,
leading me into a new tomorrow

It wasn't how I imagined—
    touching to a place of chance
  out of my world
       part of my world
 next to my heart, pulling my tears
   changing conceptions of loves

It wasn't how I planned;
   working up ideas,
      one phrase fitting with the other : overlapping
  two brains
       seeing through the same eyes—
 one soul, walking two paths
It wasn't what I felt could take place—
    charmed like a snake
       at my own front door;

 by piercing, insistent,
intelligent, colorful, direct—
      passions plays,

It wasn't what I dreamed
   but more than plans or images or thoughts
      Cutting a bargain with some
        different god
I kneel, and search for the light inside myself
      that brought you home.

SMOKING

Many things I notice about cigarettes—
since I never sucked on one before now,
alone, with your pack of camel
I experiment
in the aftermath of love with you
like a lonely teenager
with her first evil secret
lips close in on the softness of the paper

This cigarette has no filter
and (just imagine)
the smoke can glide through the screen
and six flights up from this downtown hotel
go out into the world and forget
the lips that let it forth;
and while you sleep, I guess that I could
take the end of this cigarette—
(which suddenly fills me with strange pleasure)
and I could touch the edge of those cheap
tan curtains,
could set this room ablaze and end this world
we are beginning for ourselves

love and loneliness inside one single drag.

But your smooth lips yawn in ignorance,
and we have taken and trusted one another—
so, I, like a woman,
am not disposed to the crime, and the cigarette
-my only lingering sin—
stays tamed inside my fingers,
the room lacks your chatter—
though you reel the curtains in with every snore,

the only heat now rising
is from the tar of the streets below,

in the absence of embrace
I continue my novel endeavor—
learning reluctantly to inhale—
talking as great smokers do,
with their smoke;
it curls, it touches the air
it cries, "I loved you."

it makes me remember your lips on mine—
one tear streams down, defiant—
burning through my cheek
one credit for a new experience on earth.

I let the smoke out through the screen,
To save my heart, I crush the talker flat,
red rimmed from the haze
my eyes turn, reaching you,
where, naked on the bed your soul—
lies mingled in the ashes
and the air.

MOTHER STORIES

the lady leaves me lifeless
stiff clothing mars her
suspicion rules her from her belly—
all her kisses pinch

I've walked the thin ice of her trust
like a no-good Eskimo
toting the cluttered anatomy
of a baby duck.

why does she answer me
with broken hopes and
prehistoric
remedies?

THE TREE FELLER

You can come around
    like that with your hack saw
  and chopping instruments;
and tell me it's cracked and a hazard
     and the city deems it public nuisance
but when you chop it, and send the grinders
  see how the birds feel
    and what the squirrels are doing

and how my heat bills go up in summer;
  and that was there in my mother's
    childhood
      and wasn't just about saving money
it was privacy and scenery just
  outside the window,
  it was yearly blooms and
    steady yard falls—
exercise no one minded to do.

Back when you called the bank and
  they answered you in person,
before the city kept reminding you
     you just own the shack on the dirt—
  they own the dirt and land around

Now, you tree fellers are alike—
  and there are more of you feeding
    on what I had to be proud of
      eating me out of tree and grass,

moving me out like a possum
    in the pool
so you can come and have your party
  inside the life I worked so hard for.

RENOVATIONS

the stores are closing down
in the shopping center

empty plate glass windows
stare out
all board and tile now
waiting for the cranes
to rip out last remembrances
before the new mall

little boys run by
shuffling loose pieces
along remaining sidewalk
then flying off
on their two wheeled
chrome-spoked bicycles.

old women tuck their hands
from bareness
into paper thin pockets
watching the crumbling 5 and 10
while waiting on buses.

MORNINGS' MAGIC

Learn from the magic of the morning, little one
    keep your eyes open wide
Watch as the spider spins her webbing, one by one
    don't let life pass you by
And there is magic everywhere
    from a star to a cricket
      moon to a meadow,
        tangled weeds to thicket—
everywhere, like morning is the magic,
    everyday in this world.

And to the morning skies
    cast your dreams of yesterday
    you just have to try
      what you want will pass your way.
What you believe is everything
    from a smile to a heart ache
      wish to a whisper
    miracles to earthquakes
and if you can touch the morning
    each night, deep in peace, you'll sleep

Give like the golden light of morning
    little one, not a sunbeam is free
      you will find if you live with love
    you'll have won all that you hope to be—
And from the morning air
    take your courage and your heart—
      take on all you dare—every bird song
  is your start
And in the magic of the morning
    keep believing in the world.

SIX DAYS IN PARIS, TONIGHT

Walk along the streets,
I hear your music in my mind,
see your hands at the piano and
it's hard to draw the line—

Remembering every cafe light;
our walks along the Seine—
although I could not speak the language well,
it's clear you were a friend

but I was dreaming
something quite American
some happy ending, before we made the start
and like a dream
you made it seem more beautiful
you were so easy on the heart

Close your eyes, hold me tight
I'm spending six days in Paris, tonight

Live the simple life,
or let adventure burn my eyes—
doesn't matter win or lose
in looking back, I realize
Please forgive this fantasy
in wanting us to stay

I feel the fires warmth, as I must watch the night
turn into day
and I'll be dreaming

something quite American
some happy ending, before we made the start
and like a dream you made it seem

more beautiful
you were so easy on the heart

Close your eyes, hold me tight
I'm spending six days in Paris, tonight

Like a blooming flower
colors of my life will shine
in reflection of the spirit
when our love was new and fine

Through a tapestry of autumn leaves
chased across the sky
no single memory will hold us down;

the future's in our eyes

and I'll stop dreaming
something quite American
some happy ending before we made the start
and like a dream you made it seem more beautiful
you were so easy on the heart

so close your eyes, and hold me tight
I'm spending six days in Paris, tonight.

LEAVES

Leaves come down
like tides of slanted tears
released from bondage to

the tree

free
to spin and toss
and crumble back to earth

the season's careless birth
a gold and scarlet

anarchy
that my foot dispenses
with a kick

And in the empty limbs
are diplomatic birds
arranging their last flight patterns

signaling the end of anything

warm
I am thinking, as I rake the leaves
that I'm like trees
all my children and my brilliance spent

pulled open
and in need of snow blind
covers

or someone's sympathetic tenderness.

I'M A TENNIS RACKET

Ever since you got me that racket
   I've been driving funny—

No more depression—
   I just rent a court
     At 20 bucks an hour
   And have it out with a ball machine
Suddenly all my thoughts are white
(though I occasionally dream of lobbing
     Andre Agassi in the locker room—)

I think of all I missed
   When I didn't make the tennis team
 In high school—
   Tennis elbow, bald sneakers
     And grimy beads of sweat

Between muscular toes,
   You may think I'm slow
   But I haven't learned to « follow through » yet
I have six o'clock confused with 12 o'clock
    So, if you ever decide
     I'm still worthy of competition
(in this game you forced on me—because
  there was a special at the club, and you wanted
   to show off my breasts)
just get your gear together
   and come down to court seven
 and I'll love you
   right off the face of professional sporting
because, ever since you got me that
     tennis racket
my life's become one big Forest Hills debacle—
   complete with sexy ball boys.
               Wow...Is this fulfillment!

FIRESIDE CHATS

Wood crumbles down
    like romance, burned beyond a recognition
   kisses, inefficient in their
     un-electricness fade
into these idling moments

embers in the fireplace
   at the chair side of our holiday thoughts, thus
   low heat spans the room
  churning my righteous insides;

curdling the concept of love
    into a bad milk, in the blink of Christmas bulbs

Something falls, delicate and glasslike
   from the tree,
though my imaginary furniture
    is all I can hear breaking;
      glasslike fixtures
  that my soul carved
from the ice of your heart.

Re-glowed, triumphant
   you comfort yourself, as burnt as the ashes
  evaporating even my last tear of wine

I sink in the carpet, like memory
   and sleep with our blanket of shadows

THE BLACK SQUIRREL

a black squirrel runs
across a plot of grass
   in front of the geology building

black squirrels might some day
be extinct.
Still, she carries, acorn in mouth—
the grace of a mid-summer afternoon

pausing, she angles her tail at me
almost winking,
like a concerned and wise
parent saying,
"Why are you sitting alone
   on a bench, contemplating nature?"
Evening is nearing, poems are fruitless—
It will soon be cold.
you really should be gathering
acorns in your mouth
to store for nesting and
   for feeding your children.

THE CAT

I'll open the window, it's cool
    let your meows out, Symphonia

between you spiny teeth
    the word rings forth:
you want to leave,
      pawing by the door,
for your freedom

cat

and you'll bounce feather light
    into the grass, sniffing through
        the gardens
Beethoven in your eardrums
    —from my stereo; following you—

as I dirge on my computer,
    running out of images
        as carefree as your stretching.

Back inside, you play with shadows
    as if they hold no danger of attack, Symphonia

while I scamper frantically about the rooms—
    turning off more lights
    foraging from wall

    to unfinished wall
        for the courage to seize the morning
  and the phone bill

with that self same purr of satisfaction

and how will you answer me
when the print cartridge runs out
     at midnight on Saturday;

or the computer freezes up, Symphonia?

—I own nothing but a down payment
    on the couch
  where you crevice your

    silken, shined body,
       and fall asleep.

PURPLE ROOT BEER

Sitting under black light
   sipping by the door
back against the paisley wall
   mattress on the floor

Who'd of thought this little ring
   would leave a girl this way
she's alone, while he's next door
   getting blown away

Sprays of bubbly drink with ice—
   Posters in strange light
After eight, she plays another
   purple root beer night

Eighteen years and fuzzy dreams
   She tries to hold on tight
No place to go, where she'd be safe
   This purple root beer night.

SUBURBAN POLAR BEAR

squeeze packed into pile,
cold sneaks, belly level into
soft, once sleeping contours
I proceed
intruding on this bloodless freeze
(wishing I could ski, in glamour
of the season)
the only thing protruding is my nose,
now finding a small dog—
who can not smell me through the pile
but tries anyway
soon we both return unbothered on our rounds
two non aggressive strangers with
a lot of talk.
—and where next?!
my feet are stubborn (or catalytic)
and we're on past tinseled doorways,
curb stacked greens and warm
lit, china case windows
assembled for Suburban Polar Bears
who listened for the first blue chirp
through pile.

SHIP OF LOVE

Early in the evening he goes dancing—
he's looking sweet
he goes alone, and hopes for an attraction

The music is a mist of beer and laughter—
lights make every eye, a silver smile
he won't pick anyone,
he waits for her approaching
in a little while

Dance away in silence tender stranger,
love for what you are and be a dove;
The world is crying for a softer morning,
no fools are left to board

this ship of love.

Drowning hearts are sinking all around him
everybody
but he'd like to think
he'll find the one's who's right
but who can tell what heartbreak he's romancing?

Heart to heart he holds her very tenderly
and so it's very clear, very clear
she feels the same for him
but is it that, or is it just illusion?

Dance away in silence tender stranger
love for what you will and be a dove
the world is crying for a softer morning
no fools are left to board

this ship of love

Luck was not his lady in the daylight
Mr. Moon left every kiss behind
the girl he thought she said she'd stay til morning
but it's hard to read the signs

He rises from the bed and gathers roses
that have gently fallen from her hair,
upon his floor, and through the morning fog—
a dream love lost, and nothing more

Dance away in silence, tender stranger
love for what you are and be a dove
The world is crying for a softer morning
No fools are left to board

this ship of love

SEPARATION

Take the memories off the wall
    And put them in their place
Though your soul is feeling small
    A calmness rules your face

The old wall clock is stiffly posed
    Once served—once paced for you
The frame and hands like yours lay still—
    Love's unchecked power is through

Close objects don't pretend to care
    They follow packed and sealed
Not knowing how to mend, they spur
    The hurt they help reveal

You close the door and turn the key
    Though remnants in your heart
Remember every turn of chance
    Where separation starts.

UMBRELLAS IN THE SUN

Here in the land of eternal summer
   Where a tan can cover your blemishes
   Where I wear my umbrella in the sun to walk

When the yellow in the sky burns the tops of heads

Here where the seasons no longer define themselves—
   A brief encounter with Indian summer
     A cold snap two weeks in February
   And blistery summer for as long as you remember—

  Stores that open and close within hours or days
     A month or two
Brilliantly conceived. Bankrupted by the climate

  Contacts washed away, eroded, if you are
    not constantly on the beach
   trying to hold the water,

Umbrellas in the sun, that wait for rain
   Blinded only by sun

     Umbrellas shielding tears
   Where palm trees and transient flesh
      Reign supreme

HOMESPUN VIEW

I laugh at the trains
   from the fire escape
 three flights up I feel safe
between the stacks of empty gin bottles
     a former tenant, must have drank
 many a lonely city night

But today the sunshine is bright
   the cold air's exciting
 while the iron wrought railings shed
green paint chips; I'm reminded I don't care
     I'm too light to bother about the wetness
        at my feet
 through a faulty old pair of your boots

One part mud mixes with snow and sloshes down the roof
     onto my face, so I move back:
 humbled by nature

back into your junk room
   standing now in line with your skies,
 sister to the old Heath radio
you brought from Michigan

things you can't bring yourself to
   part with

because you are a blue-eyed, homespun gypsy
   a wavy haired blonde pack rat
     and when the door clenches shut

I become part of your arms and
   your limbs
     as you climb out of your lineman boots

and into me, pulling me down for a look
   at your generous white teeth

 the day and I talk you over,
   we forgive the highway etched into your hands
     in bed, with the gypsy we love and understand

THE DISGUISE

death was not the end
    as I would have hoped

 it comes in small, dense packages
    of what can't be—

then the day you kissed
    the day you touched
        inside of me, one moment freed

death fakes with lovely afternoons
    and sleepless nights
  it echoes in familiar, re-run fights
     a glimmer of an earthly peace and lifelong rights
and swindles
    patients
 pilling up to fend if off

and wanders
 through my heart, alone
 when love is gone

it prays to sink the weak
    and gently bring them home

and goes like want to
    grab the need—not meeting one

and chortles like a jester
    caught in his own traps
       and jokes and lies
  with lacy thighs

    and tightened straps

but for the preparation, life long
    we'll be glad

for when the body stops
    we are no longer sad

no tears to fall
  or heart to break
    or road to hoe

Death wraps us all in velvet
    and with artist skill—
       presents us in full color

as we've seemed to be—

    completely still.

RIVERSIDE

I'll never go back to the riverside
    the child that I was before,
For the reeds that grow, by the river's edge
    have taken the place of the shore.

And the sun above, beats down on me
    from his big blue brother sky—
with no sympathy for what I've come to be
    or what I might be by and by

And I might have known just sunshine,
    but I ran with the wind and the rain—
and the water swims with a million things
    I can never hold on to again.

So take me not down that riverside
    where we went yesterday,
where cares of time, were down the line
    and I lived my life in play.

WELL PRESERVED

this dewy-eyed girl
      of twenty-five is following me around,
   she's amazed at the lack of lines
        around my eyes

or the firmness left on my thighs;

   She's lithe and lovely,
and for awhile I flatter myself
    knee deep in discussion of narrative creations
       properly punctuated:

using mine as example—

and thought at first my smarts,
     a mental magnetism
         —accomplishment beyond the physical
  that makes her flag me so—respect in spades

But one day I stopped to query her
    her words had more to tell,

it was least of all my brains
   for which I'd won Nobels

it's just the lack of fallen jowls
    she said, "You've aged so well!"

BEHIND BINOCULARS

Step out for a look at the sky,
    daylight in phosphorescence
  makes this road seem
      like an endless colored motor oil ribbon

mirroring car break lights
    like red pictures, perfectly captured
      in pools of still mud
making this atmospheric event

    a holiday in North America

fools with binoculars
    watch the moon slide its face
      near the sun

and in cold places,
    the trench coat of winter, turns strange
      and more merry
  slipping off, like the crystal encasements
    of ice on the slim, slackened brown
      fingers of trees

swift melting winters,
    and warmer climate respites
  both celebrate
    visual powers of the universe,
      unusual lighting by God:

the eclipse.

SCENTS

Perfume makes me dizzy
in the absence of your embrace
the clink of busy words
ties down my brain

the flattery and drinks
make empty moments

so I am not sorry you left
your cigars
or the history of your heart

I am sorry I have to live
exiled as a friend

and that in the end, it seems
we kept such fortress round our dreams.

CARNIVAL RAIN

"Daddy, I said
   we're moving too fast
this car's made of steel
   wheels are brass
feel's like I'm falling
  looking down from here"

He just laughed
  as he squeezed my shoulder—
"Grow up girl, as you grow older

Sometimes, life's a train
  run away car
through the carnival rain
cool, hard, carnival rain"

I got right off that loop de loop
   feet like rubber,my gut like soup
  thrill so empty
    like my pockets of coins

There's a man there
   tattered jeans
"Spare me a dime, if you can
    baby, please
gotta ride that train
  I gotta taste for the carnival train
cool, hard, rush my brain."

So let the rain pour down
   Fill your hungry heart
And if you can't hold on, step aside

There's others who'll take the ride
   on the carnival train

Went to school
  but wasn't clear

reasons, Daddy sent me there
all I remembered
   were tattered jeans

Poor boy took me by the hand
   "Let's go take a ride
   and I'll show you a man"

It was like the train
   riding all night in
The carnival rain
   Cool, hard, carnival rain

Sometimes we're looking
   to catch the prize
all done up, like fireflies
  crashing through the night
drifting to the ground
   end in pieces
like a part of your heart

All alone now
   with a child, but no man
feet on the ground
   but I don't understand
why it's like falling
just looking down at him
No ones laughing
   Or squeezing my shoulder
Can't get used to
   growing older

Sometimes life's a train
   Runaway far on the carnival train
Cool, hard carnival rain

WHEN I THINK OF YOU

Long night,
  can't you feel it
pushing though your life

Stay safe,
  you can't deal with
all your pain and strife

All the love you're craving
    past the point of saving

  When I think of you
    when I think of you
      when I think of you

My hands
  hold the answer—
lose yourself to dreams

Choose to, stay and dance
   for some girl
you'll never see

Oh all the love you're killing
  if you were only willing

When I think of you
  when I think of you
    when I think of you

Crying for your body
  when I'm all alone
wondering what to do
    to make you know
I'd take you home

No cure for the fever
  and still no time for me
hesitation drives me crazy, got to
  set you free

All's left, the knowing
  there can be no joy
Fools heart, never showing

Love for you's a toy
Oh all the love you're killing
  If you were only willing

When I think of you
  When I think of you
    When I think of you

RIVALS

Junior pumps calf taut speed
into the pedals of his bike

charging the hill
thrusting out his chin guard
to the inevitable peak

over which, the big guys
surpass with their motorized
bikes

leaving him in a glint of chrome

looking after them
and for his pride he sighs

he's barred from competition
with those four wheeled motored
magsters
that facelessly inhibit him
from victories at age 10

but on the speedway
it's okay
Junior has the choice of fates
before it's just too late

Junior's young
many a young one's
mechanically wound and sprung

a mini Mario Andretti.

THE DUTIES OF A QUEEN

It takes a very special mind
    to run a kingdom,
And so I find, I'm so inclined
    to rule the world I sing of—
war and taxes, great depressions,
    once a king would carry—
but now he's gone, god rest his soul
    and I've no time to tarry,

they took his life, barbarians
    by poisoning the wine—
now, I'm much less gregarious
    but still have bills to sign

so bring the news of battlefield—
    of dragons, world's unseen
I'll gratefully take the mystery and
    the duties of a queen

Once, when I was innocent,
   It wasn't half as fun
I had no cause to curse or yell—
   for all my work was done
      by maids and husband, lords and ladies;
         kitchen help, magicians
I never knew what I could do
   til I made the decisions

and with a heavy burden now to conquer day, by day
   the petty squabbles, crimes, disasters
     I can't help but say
Bring on the headache of the crown
   I'm not what you'd call green
     I gratefully take the misery and the duties of a queen

Alas, sometimes I'm lonely here
    Upon my single throne
 No manly arms to comfort me,
    To melt this heart of stone—
But when the world
   lays at your feet.
       How can you feel—alone?

And with an eager step I go
   my scepter in my hand
     with every stride of majesty

my presence ever grand—
  towards kings and kingdoms
    third dimensions,
feared and fearless, strong and tearless
  holding all the power
     with the chance to come to flower with
  in the duties of a queen!

ENTER MY SOUL

Drawing circles on your skin—
    wasn't hard to take me in,
        in the starting days, a lover's haze

but like a lightening storm with flashing lights;
    love changes form

Into my heart, enter my soul
    You'll never know til' I let it show
  in my dreams, the things you'd see
      if you'd touch me
        in my mind, in my heart
    in my mind in my heart,
        in my mind, in my heart, through my soul

Chasing money these hungry hours
    shallow kisses, forgotten powers
        and how they used to dance
  in that new romance
    but I still feel the fire
      soon to lift us higher

Into my heart, enter my soul
  You'll never know, til I let it show
  In my dreams, these things you see,
    if you touch me
  in my mind, in my heart

   in my mind, in my heart
      in my mind, in my heart, through my soul

You say we can't live on dreams—
   I ask, who lives without them
   Baby, mine are loud as screams
     Full of wonder in my mind,
   Thunder in my heart;
      Fire in my soul, my love
        My love

Take the hammer and take the nails—
   tender warriors never fail
And when they pull the wall
   enjoy the fall

and we still feed the fire
   soon to life us higher

into my heart, enter my soul
  you'll never know, til I let it show
    in my dreams the thing you see

if you touch me
   in my mind, in my heart
      in my mind, in my heart

in my mind, in my heart, through my soul
   my love.

FOUR WALLS AND A CEILING

everywhere I look, four walls
    and ceiling—
  filled with dreaming of the sky

candlesticks and books, it's such a funny feeling
    lights play tricks upon the eyes

shadows fade away to star shine
     they grow too large to disappear from sight
hard to settle down, don't know how

I'd rather fly with creatures in the night

storms are brewing here, I know
    in your sad eyes
  that your heart is far away

but you must take heart
    morning brings a new sky—
      celebrating a new day

seasons fade away and time flies
    no one knows what's happening inside

the world where you live, it calls out
   close your eyes, and wish
      then say goodbye

everywhere I look four walls and a ceiling
     you and I

NAKED FEATHERS

Driving through the rain
   with sun on my brain
down the inter-state line-
Flyin on home
   where I wind up alone and,
then try to unwind

think I came here for the weather
  only a soul flies away
      on naked feathers , naked feathers

Used to play wild
  with my inner child
there's so much to see
Passage of time, you
  can forget all the signs
soon, you're no longer free

think I'll stay here for the weather
  only a soul flies high
   on naked feathers, naked feather

Green, green parrots
  high up in the tree
talking like they'll never stop—
  living the way they did
   hundreds of years ago
carving their niche at the top
   so light, and unfettered
      on naked feathers, naked feathers

Beach where we walked
   kissed and we talked
 so different now
marble and glass
   gone are things of the past
  under toe, under plow

Since I stayed here for
  the weather, baby my soul still cries
     on your naked feathers, naked feathers

GIVE ME BACK MY HEART

I know that you're gone
   so plain to see
  no chains to bind us, forever free

But now I just go mad, babe
  in the middle of the night
could've left just one thing
  and then things would be alright

Keep all the love
  you did from the start
one of these days

Give me back my heart
  give me back my heart

Know I'm not dreaming
  there's no dream to hold
I'm lost in the daylight
  at night things are cold

You say it's over
  think you're so smart
so one of these days

Give me back my heart

Give me back my heart
Like a restless rider
  On a carousel
Or a lonely penny in
  A wishing well

I could fight but there's nothing to win

  I might end if we meet again

One day I'll be moving
   not stare into space
 leave you behind me, get out of this place

I get the feeling you still hold the cards
Your ace to my joker—
  the odds, they're just too hard

You take all the kisses
  you have from the start

Just one of these days

   Give me back my heart
    give me back my heart

EVERY LANGUAGE

Take some time, while the sun still shines
   while your heart still beats
  never cry defeat

To love your neighbors all
   so that every one will shine
think of the joys you would find

Listen in every language
   every word of love

learn not to take for granted—
   that's enough
listen in every language
  listen in every language

Keep the peace, let your fingers reach
   where the road is rough
  fill the empty cups
   for every hungry child
for those who lose their way

show them a brighter day

Listen in every language
  every word of love

learn not to take for granted—
   that's enough
listen in every language
   listen in every language

In this world
  every boy, each girl
  has a special dream
   and so real it seems
to see beyond the clouds

to keep their people free
  as far as the eye can see

We've got to listen
   in every language
every word of love
don't ever take for granted—that's enough

Listen in every language
   Listen in every language.

THE UN-OPENING

layer by layer
   —forcing open packages
     near the heart

we bend
  and strip our consciousness
     another time
to that bare and

     quivering place
of confession—
laughing in a land of secrets
    we've defied.

cash in hand for the goods of love
   —pirates of a darker age
     exchanging treasure chests

while down deep
    crying for lost virginity (a thousand times)
  for quiet stories
    of mythic loneliness
   remembering
a sacred place, with something locked away
     for only one

deep and hidden
    is my heart for you
  waiting for the pirates to pass over—
     the un-opening.

GETTING OFF THE GROUND

Don't thank yourself for looking back
or counting friends you've won
the next step is the hardest yet
with nowhere left to run
and the biggest remedy of fear
is one that's never found
until you've learned the simple trick
of getting off the ground

Those kings and paupers play for money
lose and bet the same
don't think you're special, born of angels
you love and bleed the same
and smallest feet can swifter pass
by making smaller sounds
and launching every ounce they have
for getting off the ground

Special Thanks to the following artists for their imaginative contributions:

Illustrator Theresa Solotoff for sketches accompanying "Gone Frogging," "Ides," and others.

Illustrator Christopher Paul Bostick for sketches accompanying "A Cowboy Named Dave," "Put it in the Music," and others.

Photographer Elyse Friedman-Brunt for cover photograph as well as interior photos for "Pigeons," "Six Days in Paris," and others; as well as her help with graphic layout and design throughout the book.

Naked Feathers was enriched by your artwork. Thanks, DB

To my mother, Emily Bostick for her great imagination, and enthusiasm in support of my creative self and her poem in this book, "Only Girl".

978-0-595-40083-6
0-595-40083-3

Printed in the United States
202687BV00004B/1-39/A